Colonel Vaughan Witten PhD

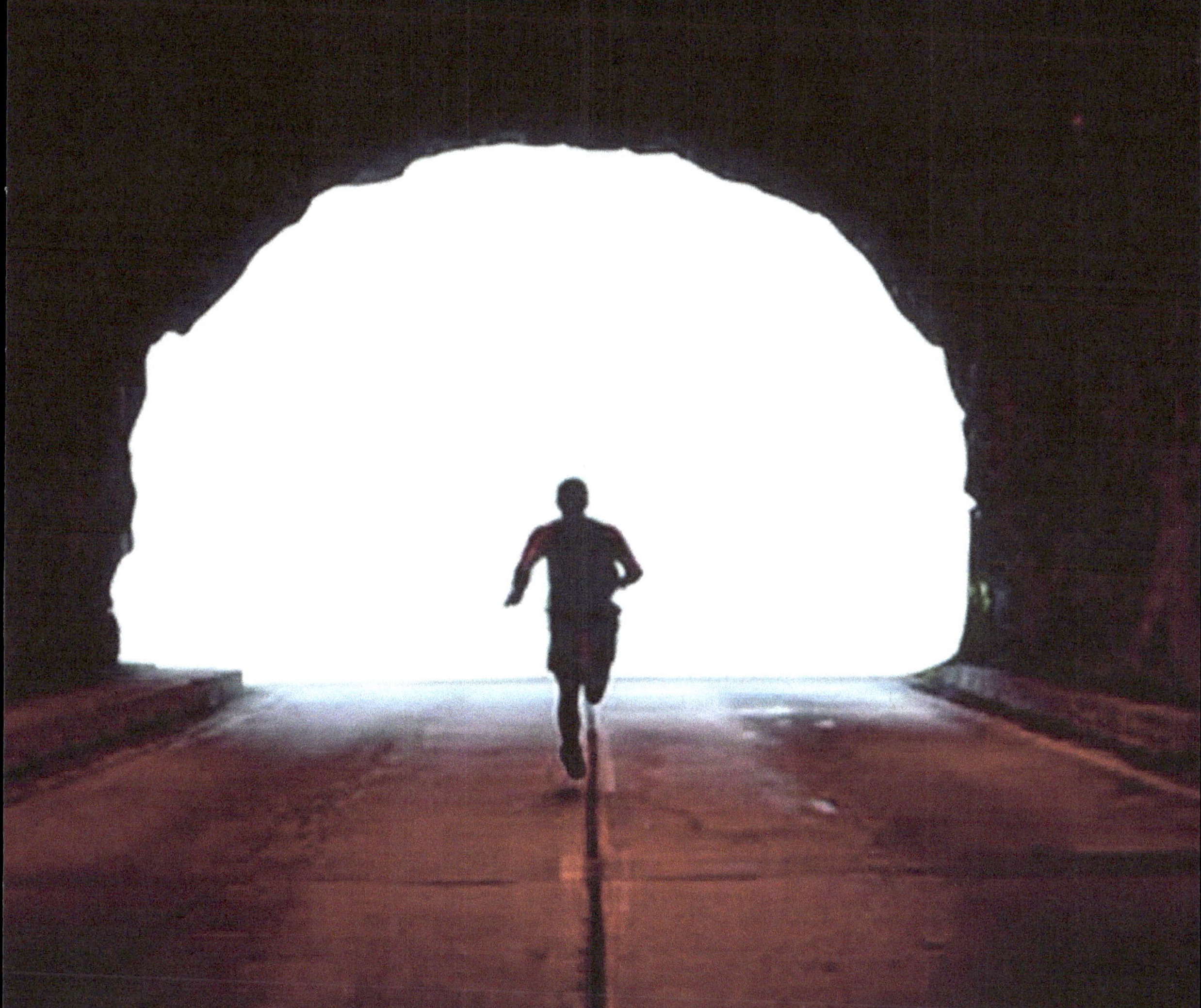

BLACK ESCAPE FROM FREEDOM

The Fallacy of Victimism, and Resulting Self Defeating Behavior and Avoidance of Responsibility

Copyright © 2024 by Colonel Vaughan Witten PhD
All rights reserved. No part of this publication may be reproduced, distributed, or transmitted in any form or by any means, including photocopying, recording, or other electronic or mechanical methods, without the prior written permission of the copyright owner and the publisher, except in the case of brief quotations embodied in critical reviews and certain other noncommercial uses permitted by copyright law. For permission requests, write to the publisher, "Attention: Permissions Coordinator," to the address below.

Studio of Books LLC
5900 Balcones Drive Suite 100
Austin, Texas 78731
www.studioofbooks.org
Hotline: (254) 800-1183

Ordering Information:
Special discounts are available on quantity purchases by corporations, associations, and others. For details, contact the publisher at the address above.

Printed in the United States of America.

ISBN-13:   Hardcover   978-1-964864-24-2

Library of Congress Control Number: 2024913265

CONTENTS

From The Pages

Of

THE BLACK ESCAPE FROM FREEDOM

Escape from Freedom aka Fear of Freedom1

Escape from Freedom-Black American.-4

The National and Moral Dilemma.-9

Victimism and the Victim Mentality.-12

Sympathy.-13 Learned Behavior.-14

Inability to Control Emotions.-16

Heart vs Mind Thinking.-19

Philosophical Rivalry WEB Du Bois vs Booker T Washington.-22

Pyrrhic Victory-Winning the Battle and

Losing the War.-27

The Boogieman.-32

American Black Leadership and Slavery .34

Old Wine in New Bottles.-37
Hatred and Confusion.- 38

Boogieman Article.-40

El Coco.-41

Hatred and Confusion Article.-42

Black American Leaders-Picures.-43

Map of Free and Slave States 1861.-44

Africa during the Slave Trade.-45

Nat Turner Slave Rebellion.-46

Denmark Vesey Planned Insurrection.-49

Slavery Pictures.-50

Ku Klux Klan.-52

Black Codes-Laws.-54

Jim Crow Laws.-55

Booker T Washington.-56

W.E.B. Du Bois.-58

Marcus Garvey.-60

Thurgood Marshall.-62

Martin Luther King.-54

Malcolm X.-66

Freedom in World History.-68

U.S. Freedoms.-73

What Does "Freedom" Mean.-75

Rights Reserved.-81

References.-82

BLACK ESCAPE FROM FREEDOM: The Fallacy Of Victimism , and Resulting Self Defeating Behavior and Avoidance of Responsibility.

1

Escape From freedom, aka, the fear Of freedom is a concept presented by German psychologist Erich Fromm, first published in the United States by Farrar & Rinehart in 1941. Fromm explores humanities shifting relationships with freedom, in particular regard to the personal consequences of its absence. He focuses primarily on the psychosocial conditions of society that facilitates crime, disorder, dictatorships, hopelessness poverty, dependence and other factors that contribute to the despair and apathy that limits or cripples ones desire to be free. Fromm distinguishes between "freedom from" (negative freedom) and "freedom to" (positive freedom). Freedom" from" refers to social emancipation from restrictions such as conventions placed on individuals by other individuals or institutions, such as slavery. This is the type of freedom typified as being fought for historically. To escape bondage, of the physical self. The concept of" Freedom to", however is to control and abuse others who are powerless to defend their dignity, and world view, or refers to the authenticity to submit to an authoritarian system that replaces the old order with another, different in appearance but with an identical function for the individual: that is to eliminate uncertainty by prescribing what to think and how to act. Fromm's thesis contains a paradoxical idea that people struggle for freedom then struggle with freedom. They really don't know what to do with it when they get it.

For Fromm freedom brings with it uncertainty, whereas the lack of freedom brings certainty and COMFORT.(Ibid) While freedom seems appealing when people are not free, it brings a sudden and unexpected responsibility(Fromm, Ibid). This leads to an anxiety that can simply be overwhelming from a psychological point of view. As a result, people make choices to relieve themselves of anxiety (Fromm, Ibid). Of Fromm's three primary principles that affect choice in the escape from freedom, the concept of destruction appears to be the most applicable to my hypothesis of applying his idea to the plight of most black American's in the present United States of America, (Witten 2017) . He continues that people without an authoritarian or structured system such as the family, which many young blacks do not have, are dysfunctional (my emphasis), or have no normal group norm to conform to and thus often self- destruct. This is manifested in low self- esteem and self- destructive behavior like crime, drug addiction, suicide, entitlement ideation and murder,(Fromm 1941). He, Fromm concludes that what- ever negates the results of these destructive choices are considered preferable to the anxiety and uncertainty that freedom brings.

Escape From Freedom: Black Americans
Although Fromm's thesis can be applied to several socioeconomic, racial, or cultural situations and oppressive dilemmas-it can and does fit well as a depiction or at least a partial explanation for the maladaptive behavior of a significant portion of the Black

American population living an impoverished life in the ghetto, and many middle class children contaminated by the cultural contamination of lawlessness , disrespect for self and others, apathy, low self-esteem, self- entitlement, black on black crime and murder.

Now that America has produced a nanny welfare state of giving away the store to everyone who has a problem; disease, loss of job, handicap, poor health, needs an Obama phone or food stamps, wants free school lunches, ,subsidized housing, fake disability claims, broken toe nails or   any other freebies available on a whim or plea no matter how deceitful they may be in many cases—is it any wonder that so many people have their hand out, with the tax payer carrying this burden that keeps adding to our 20 trillion dollar debt? Unfortunantly many are comfortable in the cocoon of welfare and the security and certainty of a government check- thus avoiding , fleeing the alternant choice of responsibility and independence necessary to be FREE. A government check every month is too powerful a tonic to discard and move to freedom. To do so would mean getting up at 5:00 am every-day for work, have to pay taxes, no EBT card, obey the law, cook healthy meals, cut back on the fat burgers, register car on time, stop driving on expired licenses. Also protect one's health against sugar related diseases such as diabetes, and high blood pressure that is prevalent among about 80% of individuals receiving treatment for dialysis and many having obesity related problems and high blood pressure even before leaving high school.

These along with about any other disease you can even think of especially heart disease and cancer. Yes white trailer trash have many of these same problems, such as weak ethics and mores, but that's a topic for another conversation or book. This one is about the self-destruction of the <u>Black race.</u>

We have been mesmerized by the liberal democratic "progressive" cultural movement that pushes and praises same sex marriage, abortion, transgender bathrooms, marijuana, and other godless things, plus failure to properly educate their children, lack of discipline and fathers in the home that we have become conditioned to our situation to the degree that we think it is normal. This desensititation has chipped away at our humanity as a nation where human life has lost it's value and lawlessness, deceit, robbery, lying and murder is normalized and accepted as just the way it is and will be. We cry and complain,blame the white man for everything, failing to realize that we are our own worst enemy. The white man knows it and just laughs, because he doesn't mind our cultural suicide, example 5,000 shootings and 762 murders in Chicago in 2016 with 95% of those being black on black. We have drank a toxic brew "koolaid" of progressive liberalism and thus planted the seeds of our demise, which now we are reaping the harvest.

    The sad thing is we are not even aware of our slide into hell or conscious of the huge danger we're in. The Chinese, Indians, Vietnamese, Hispanics, even Bangladeshes and others will replace us at the table in spite of all the suffering and sacrifice of our ancesters ; and the race baiting ,shallow rhetoric of Al Sharpton and Jesse Jackson, President Obama' failed effort as the messiah and all the crying, complaining , and flailing against the establishment will not save us.

Our National Moral And Financial Dilemma
    Although America is currently a rich and powerful nation, we are on a steady, rapid, economic, fiscal, moral and ethical decline. Our military is our most effective, strong, and honorable institution, of which I belong and was my escape if you will from the coal mines of West Virginia. I love West Virginia but didn't want to spend the best part of my life digging coal deep under the mountains. In fact the military remains one

of the primary ways that young black men can escape poverty but many have no interest, lack the discipline and a clean criminal record. But even a good military and loads of bombs and bullets can not save a nation. Ask about ancient Rome, Greece, Egypt, and other empires why they fell. It was not about a weak military per se, but more from internal weakness, selfishness, pursuit of pleasure and loss of integrity and ethics and crushing debt. Sound familiar—sounds like us doesn't it. We are fast approaching bankruptcy with a $20,000,000,000,000 national debt, and a half trillion $ budget deficit each year. Our trajectory is unsustainable, but we just keep kicking the can down the road. We will soon join the P.I.G.S.S nations of Portugal, Italy, Greece, Spain, Syria and more recently Venezuela- who can't pay their bills and in some cases can't feed their people. Like the PIGSS ,America's gravey train is headed for a derailment, with even our sacred social security being jeopardized if we continue what we are doing. In 1935 when it was started there were over 100 people paying in, to every 1 person getting a check- but now there are only 3 people paying into the program for every 1 person getting a check. It doesn't sound good does it. So as we get closer to the cliff, what will happen to those who deny reality and cling to the comfort zone of good ol Uncle Sam. What will happen to those escaping from freedom and waiting on the transfer payment?

But beyond the economic disaster looming, the moral disaster is even worse. There has been 65,000,000 babies killed by way of abortion since 1973 via the Roe vs Wade

Supreme Court decision in 1973. Blacks are 63% of all criminals in prison and jails in the U.S, 72% of all black babies are born out of wedlock, blacks are 60% more likely than Whites to have diabetes, 40% more likely to be obese, 40% more likely to have cancer , 200% more likely to have cervix or prostate cancer and 93% more likely to be murdered by another black as they are to be murdered by a white person. Is this avalance of doom and death worth fleeing from freedom into the abyss of the democrats promise of a " free lunch" and the resultant sentence of extinction. Now for the delusion of victimization as an excuse for our destructive behavior.

Victimization aka Victim Mentality
In the most general sense, a victim is anyone who experiences injury, or mis-

fortune as a result of some event or series of events,(Funk,2000). This negative experience however is insufficient for the emergence of a sense of victimization (Ibid, 2000). It has been suggested that individuals define themselves as victims if they believe that: 1 They were harmed,
2 They were not responsible for the occuring of the harmful act,
3 They were under no obligation to prevent the harm,
4 That the harm constituted an injustice.
5 That they deserve sympathy, (Ibid 2000).

Sympathy

The desire for sympathy is crucial in that the mere experience of a harmful event is not enough for the emergence of this sense of being a victim,(Funck,2000). In order to have this sense there is a need to perceive the harm as undeserved, unjust, and immoral – an act that could not be prevented by the victim- ergo the need for sympathy can then emerge.

A victim mentality may manifest itself in a range of different behaviors or ways of thinking and talking.

Blaming others for a situation that one has created or significantly contributed to. Then failing or unable to take responsibility for ones actions.

Ascribing non-existent negative intentions to other people (similar to paranoia). These people often develop convincing and sophisticated arguments in support of such ideas, which they can use to convince themselves and others of their victimized status,(Witten 2013)

Learned behavior and Transfer of Blame Victim mentality is primarily learned, for example from family members and situations during childhood. Similarly criminals often engage in victim thinking, believing themselves to be blameless and engaging in crime only as a reaction to external pressure, and that police unfairly single them out for prosecution,(Funk,2000), E Fromm: His Life and Ideas, New York, Continuum pp 169-173.

Blacks in this context seek to transfer blame which subverts their responsibility. Exacting racism as the major force behind Black tribulations and problems fosters a self defeating notion that crime, drug abuse, family disintergration, teen age pregnancy, which disrupts black communities,should be excused until white people act right and treat them better. As Eddie Murphy said, this "militant black brother stuff is not working, "(Violence Policy Center, 2014- Frederick Robinson 1991).

As long as young black males believe their shortcomings are the result of ingrained racism, their under achievement of failing to read and write, get a job, intergrate into society, obey the law-exaserbated by their victimization mentality, hatred of white people, poverty, suicide, crime, and dysfunctional families... they will continue to slide into the abyss of a hopeless and pitiful future.

Inability to Control Emotions

Tavis Smiley, a Black talk show host and liberal political activist says black people are too emotional to obey rules,(June 2007, C-Span PBS). Tons of psychological studies have resulted in outcomes that show that the average Black person has low EI-Emotional Intellegence- ie; lacks or has low ability to delay gratification, difficulty in understanding the concept of responsibility, have poor self regulation, low empathy, weak self awareness, and difficulty in controlling their emotions, Goldman 1995, Whitman et al, Wiley Online, April 2014.

Richard Lynn 2002 advances the theory that these are factors that accounts for the Black high rate of crime. Deborrah Cooper 2010 while discussing the emotionally abusive black man-postulates that both depression and obesity are at epidemic levels amongst black women in the United States and believe these afflictions are attributable to stressful interactions and relationships with black men. She continues with the hypothesis that most abusive men tend to be those that feel most powerless, least confident, and most insecure about their abilities and accomplishments. These men in the U.S., mostly black, in famlial, romantic, or social environments tend to demonstrate a marked and increased disdain and lack of respect for black women. She contends that black men present themselves,as toxic, full of rage, and project this insecurity and fear onto black women at every opportunity. Whether in public and or among strangers or romantic relationships, their communications with black women are laden with critical behavior.

It's important to impress their buddies and prove they are a man by shaming women. Deborra asserts that black men never apologize because what they do is done on purpose to break the womans spirit and gain power over her. He is initially nice to her and makes her happy, then pulls the rug out and watches her crash. Feeling confused and wounded, the woman feels guilty that she did something to make him"change", accepts the shift in blame and now he has control over her happiness. Deborrah,(Ibid).

Heart vs Mind Thinking

In humans the thought process originates in the mind or brain that is inside the head of an individual. The brain is subdivided into two major hemispheres (sides) that are connected by a bundle of nerves that tells each side what the other is doing so they remain in synch. This would be like an anatomical e-mail sent to each other. The left side is the logical planning executive that is rational and analytical-the worker if you will. It drives your car, does your taxes, pays your bills, avoids getting hit by a bus, and so on. The right side is the emotional side that is involved in creative ability, music,spatial intelligence, and dreaming among similar activities. It's also the one that flys off the handle, cusses people out, hates the police for no reason-if one does so, slaps the wife if dinner is burned, or shoots people that they may feel has offended them. Now this is not a crazy side per se, for most normal people it is under the control of the left side to a large degree, but it can take temporary control over the left under emotion. This is especially so if the person has weak ethical and moral values structured into their personality, by way of lack of early family love in childhood, lack of feeling safe, insecurity, low self esteem, poor health care, poverty, and feelings of abuse and abandonment among other factors. Now, NOT everyone who develops in a dysfunctional environment is affected to the degree that leads to criminality or irrational emotions to mask over their pain, but many are, and they manifest their discontent by lashing out at others for trivial things in order to close the hole in their soul. The heart of course does not "think", it is an organ that pumps blood through out the body delivering oxygen and nutrients to tissue and organ systems. However it has been a euphemism since the ancient Greeks for the source of feelings. Modern science has now produced more evidence that right brained thinkers are more intuitive, better at facial recognition, color recognition, more musical, better ability to read emotions, and less concerned with time or timeliness than left brain-thinkers,(Roger Sperry, 1981). There is research and anecdotal evidence that we black people in general tend to be right brain oriented. We seem to excel in music, art, singing, story telling,and reacting to ambiguous and irrelevant stimuli,(Witten, 1989). Women are also believed to be more right brained than men. This view proposes that whites excell at left brained activities, math, engineering, science, biology, logical thinking, and objective analyses. The research on dominance is inconclusive on the why . It does not appear to be biological but more a function of early childhood development, social conventions, family experiences and the overall effect of community values,(Witten,1989)

Racial Philosophical Rivalry
WEB Dubois vs Booker T Washington

The future of slaves after emancipation relied heavily on the ideas, politics, world view, and efforts of these men after 1865. Booker Talliferro Washington, 1856-1915, was born a slave in Virginia, worked in a salt mine as a youth and went to school at Hampton Institute after the civil war. In 1881 he headed theTuskegee Institute in Alabama, teaching moral instruction and industrial skills, to former slaves including thrift, construction, farming, brick mason, carpentry, math, English, writing and other practical skills necessary to make them successful. He believed economic independence and ability as productive members of society would lead to true equality and civil rights. He preached a philosophy of self help, racial solidarity and interaction with whites on a basis of accommodation.

William Edward Burghardt DuBois,1868-1963 was born in Massachusetts to a free black family. In 1885 he attended Fisk University in Tennessee where he had his first encounter with Jim Crow. He earned his PHd in Sociology from Harvard University in 1895, the first black to do so. He said NO to Booker T Washington's philosophy of the future for the Black man and maintained that education and civil rights were the only way to success. Du Bois believed Booker T's strategy would serve only to perpetuate white oppression. He proposed political action and a civil rights agenda and helped to found the NAACP. He also developed a relatively small group of college educated blacks called the "Talented Tenth" to guide the masses away from the contamination and death of the worst, (Gibson, R. 1978).

So how did this rivalry of philosophical predictions turn out 120 years later? Not so good for the Black race in my opinion, even though DuBois got much of what he wanted politically in the long run. Yes we have the civil rights act, the voting rights act, public accommodations legislation, and many other benefits like food stamps, EBT card, section 8 housing, ride in the front of the bus, affirmative actions and so on BUT what has it done for our self- worth, our independence, our ability to maintain a two parent family, our dignity, economic status, our ability to restrain our emotions in reaction to stress and frustration? Little to none in my observation. In many ways we are more enslaved now than were our forefathers and mothers and we don't even have the burden of the whip or chains. We are psychological pseudo slaves for our bodies are free but our minds are basically contaminated by a need for pity, a need for attention and approval, a need for a protector (government) a need or want of the almighty government check instead of the pursuit of independence and autonomy. Yes we are prisoners of our own making, and

refuse to acknowledge our real dilemma or dynamics of the continuing evolution to a more dismal future while our race huslers and white haters will continue to blind us and lead us away from the true equality and freedom that Booker T Washington thought we could achieve with his view of economic independence and self- help. Du Bois' concept of the talented tenth has devolved into the talented 100th and has failed to guide the masses from contamination—as he call-it. His social and political agenda failed to see the collapse of our pride, our integrity, our loss of love for each other, the loss of our desire to sacrifice our immediate pleasure for long term gain and success.
Of course we can't blame him for not anticipating the loss of the strength we once had. But yet it is what it is—as some people say. A huge part of our Black nation has sec-

cumed to the ideology of victimization and all the negative results. This delusion is fostered and perpetrated by the lame NAACP and many others of the same ilk, and thus leading us over the cliff and into the water as lemmings. The apparent victory of Du Bois is a hollow one in that the means did not validate or produce the desired ends.

PYRRHIC VICTORY

"Winning the Battle and Losing the War" In a sense the current Black American culture has disappointed and failed both Du Bois and Washington. We have not delivered their expectations in either camp. Although WEB Du Bois appears to have won *a* superficial victory in civil rights and political gains, while Booker T' views of providing independence through construction, farming, and utility education has for all intentions failed, the Du Bois view-or "victory" seems to be of a pyrrhic nature. That is, the Black race is in far much worse shape now than it was in April 1865- with four million freed slaves who had no education and no knowledge of what to do with their freedom.

    The phrase Pyrrhic victory is named for King Pyrrhus of Epirus in which he defeated the Romans at Heraclea in 280 BC and at Asculum in 279 BC, but lost so many men of his army that as he said " one other such victory would utterly undo him". Though the Romans lost more men in the battles, they had many more men to replace their losses- so one more battle with Rome had the probable effect of destroying his army. (www http://enWikapedia.org. Dec. 2016. Du Bois won his battles and appeared to have won the war, but not a lasting one. After100 years what did he or our race actually gain? It seems that we have went backwards. I would posit that we have had little effective progress in our social politics movement over Washington's utilitarian, industrial education and self help-self reliant ideaology. For all of our social and civil rights and opportunities, we have squandered and frittered away most of the advances made by our ancestors. We don't vote in numbers large enough to influence public policy, and even when we do, 90% vote in lock step blind obedience to the democrat party which takes us for granted and delivers only false promises and a politically debilitating welfare check and EBT card. We have actually digressed in our effort for a place at the table, and now grovel over the scraps from the table instead of a seat at the table. Many immigrants from all over the world come here poor, and with strong work ethics and powerful motivation pushing their drive for success, often rapidly move ahead of us and gain a seat at the table. And what is even more sad is that we often resent them for their achievements.

The 4 million slaves were much more capable, proud, resilient, hardworking, cunning, intelligent, hopeful and powerful, than we are today; with our cars, credit cards, cell phones, air conditioning, food stamps, free lunches, airplanes, EBT cards, and affirmative action. WHY? Because we have lost our way and refuse to change our course from a circular self- defeating route, to a linear straight line to success, power and Freedom. WE have lost our (raison detre), our reason to be. No purpose, just here, consuming the bounty of others, while putting nothing back into the basket. We are surviving on a treadmill menu of apathy, poverty, despair, delusion, crime, and depression. We keep doing the same, irrational things, yet expect good rational outcomes. One of the definitions of insanity is to keep doing the same thing and expecting different results. This delusion seems to be a permanent characteristic, implacable and the slippery slope to purgatory which seems more likely than not. The ball is in our court and it is not smart to punt. We must learn to play the game by the appropriate rules and do it better than our opponent-if you will. We can't play the game of checkers when everyone else is playing chess. The results will always be the outcome of failure. We actually provide a strong case of a "self- fulfilling"prophesy, acting in such a way that predicts and promotes the high probability of a negative out come that we didn't want. The fear of the Booggie man of freedom cements our wrong turn that   has led to our demise.

The Boogieman

The Boogieman or bogeyman is a common allusion to a mythical creature in many cultures used by adults to frighten children into good behavior. The monster has no specific appearance, and conceptions about it can vary from household to household. It is simply a non-specific embodiment of of a creature of terror. In some cases , the bogyman is the nickname for the Devil. Parents often tell their children that if they misbehave, the bogey man will get them. He is usually a male entity but can be female.

We have constructed in our mind that the white man is our euphemistic boogieman. The white race is foreign to us even after 152 years of emancipation. We are afraid of him, or at least we don't trust him and as in most cases, attribute evil motives and deeds to him, when it is not true. But you see that gives a foundation for blaming him for our problems and escaping our guilt for our failure to progress. You see once you have a boogieman to blame, you can seek pity, and assistance without fear of condesention, because we can now say it is not "our fault." Once this is psychologically achieved we can claim victimization status. As "victims" we are now the children being punished by the boogieman, though in our mind we have not misbehaved. This type of thinking strongly influences our motivation

to remain in our "safe" cocoon of the ghetto, with the benefits of transfer payment checks, EBT, and other social and governmental benefits , and flee from the alternative choice of escaping to FREEDOM and the dignity, self respect, independence, and self reliance that go's with it.

Sometimes when we look into a dark closet and perceive an object that we construe to be scary, it may not be the boogieman at all, it's just a Coat. Such it is with social perceptions- sometimes what we see is what it is, and nothing more.

Black leadership in the U.S. and Slavery
We have had hundreds of brave, sincere Black leaders in the past,(although some-

times misguided) who have toiled for our equality, human rights and freedom.

We have also had many opponents to that desire for freedom.

LEADERS

Nat Turner,-Slave, 1800-1831.
Denmark Vesey,- Freed Slave 1767-1822.
Marcus Garvey, Jamaican,1887-1940.
Booker T Washington,Educator,1856-1905.
WEB DU Bois, Activist, Educator,1868-1963.
Thurgood Marshall,-Supreme Court,1908-1993.
Malcolm X, Muslim Minister , 1925- 1965.
Martin Luther King, Baptist Minister 1929-1968.
Alphonso Witten, W.Va. coal miner 1913-1991.

ANTI- Black Institutions and Laws

Ku Klux Klan,1865-Present.
Jim Crow Laws,1866-1965.

Plessey vs Ferguson, 1896 "separate-equal"
1800-1866 Black Codes.
Oregon anti- Black- Laws 1844-1857
Fugitive Slave Law 1850.
1892 Democrats repealed all Republican passed Black civil rights laws when they took control of the House, Senate and the White House.

  The fight for equal rights and "real" freedom has continued from the pre emancipation days up until today. But after all this pain, blood, and sacrifice we can't seem to reap the full benefits of their toil, and we squander the opportunities given us, by our apathy, sense of entitlement, lack of respect, lack of pride, disrespect for the law, loss of love for each other, and the obsessive fear and hatred for white people. We will never actually be free until we turn from our flight FROM freedom to the flight TO freedom. We must come to realize that We are the captains of our soul and masters of our fate.

Old Wine in New Bottles

It sad to say but actually we are Quasi-Free Blacks. Yes, we have freedom of movement and can go pretty much anywhere we want, with no physical chains binding us, but we are a prisoner of our minds with not much hope of achieving the American dream. Yes a few of us have "made" it but most of us are caught in a vicious cycle of despair, crime, fear, drugs, and intolerance. We are blinded to the causation of our plight and refuse to change. We continue to pour the same old " wine "into new bottles and imagine that it tastes different.

Hatred and Confusion

Troy Williams, (2017) says Donald Trump haters have gone to great lengths to enlighten the world about America's new presidents' flaws but also unwittingly exposed their hypocricy. Hate is a very strong emotion and the hate for President Trump has made America more divided. But the haters behavior of profanity, vitriol, disrepect and vulgarity cast a strong light upon their character and are disrespecting themselves in the process. These hater's not only show hate to President Trump but also to other American's who support him. Mr. Williams cited scripture that say's "Hypocrite! First take the log out of your eye, then you will see clearly to take the speck out of your brother's eye". This is very insightful. I would suggest not to throw rocks if you live in a glass house.

To conclude, it appears that we are trapped by at least four of Sigmund Freud's fifteen psychological defense mechanism,s ie; denial, projection, displacement & rationalization . Denying or treating unpleasant thoughts, emotions, and facts as if they don't exist. Projecting or disowning ones unwanted or disliked thoughts and behaviors-attributing them to others, displacing and reducing anxiety by the transfer or "dumping" of feelings towards one person onto another eg; mad at the boss and then go home and kick the cat, and finally Rationalization or making subconscious excuses or reasons to make and justify poor behavior seem logical. Many of us prefer the false security, comfort, and day to day survival of a BIG FISH in a small Pond over being a small FISH in a BIG ocean with its relative insecurity and anxiety BUT the advantage of growth, and the potential for unlimited opportunity, advancement, wealth, and most importantly:FREEDOM.

Bogeyman

From Wikipedia, the free encyclopedia

Bogeyman (usually spelled **boogeyman** in the U.S.; also spelled **bogieman** or **boogie man**; see American and British English spelling differences), pronounced /bʊgimæn/ or /boʊgimæn/,[1] is a common allusion to a mythical creature in many cultures used by adults to frighten children into good behavior. This monster has no specific appearance, and conceptions about it can vary drastically from household to household within the same community; in many cases, he has no set appearance in the mind of an adult or child, but is simply a non-specific embodiment of terror. Parents may tell their children that if they misbehave, the bogeyman will get them. Bogeymen may target a specific mischief—for instance, a bogeyman that punishes children who suck their thumbs—or general misbehaviour, depending on what purpose needs serving. In some cases, the bogeyman is a nickname for the Devil. Bogeyman tales vary by region. The bogeyman is usually a masculine entity, but can be any gender, or simply be androgynous.

Goya's *Que viene el Coco* ("Here Comes the Bogeyman / The Boogeyman is Coming") c. 1797

Etymology

The word *bogey* is believed to be derived from the Middle English *bogge / bugge* ("hobgoblin") and is generally thought to be a cognate of the German *bögge, böggel-mann* (English "Bogeyman").[2] The word could also be linked to many similar words in other European languages: *bogle* (Scots), *boeman* (Dutch), *Butzemann* (German), *busemann* (Norwegian), *bøhmand / bussemand* (Danish), *bòcan, púca, pooka* or *pookha* (Irish), *pwca, bwga* or *bwgan* (Welsh), *puki* (Old Norse), *pixie* or *piskie* (Cornish), *puck* (English), *mumus* (Hungarian), *bogu* (Slavonic), *buka* (Russian, бука), *bauk* (Serbian), *bubulis* (Latvian), *baubas* (Lithuanian), *bobo* (Polish), *bebok* (Silesian), *papão* (Portuguese), *торбалан* (Bulgarian), Μπαμπούλας (Greek), *bua* (Georgian, ბუა), *babau* (Italian), *baubau* (Romanian), and *papu* (Catalan).[3]

A related word, *bugbear*, from *bug*, meaning goblin or scarecrow, and *bear*, was imagined as a demon in the form of a bear that eats small children, and was also used to mean a general object of dread.[4] The word *bugaboo*, with a similar pair of meanings, may have arisen as an alteration of *bugbear*.[5]

Other putative origins

In Southeast Asia, the term is popularly supposed to refer to Bugis[6] or Buganese[7] pirates, ruthless seafarers of southern Sulawesi, Indonesia's third-largest island. These pirates often plagued early English and Dutch trading ships of the British East India Company and Dutch East India Company. It is popularly believed that this resulted in the European sailors' bringing their fear of the "bugi men" back to their home countries. However, etymologists disagree with this, because words relating to *bogeyman* were in common use centuries before European colonization of Southeast Asia and it is unlikely that the Bugis would have been commonly known to westerners during that time.

El Coco

In Spain, parents will sing lullabies or tell rhymes to children, warning them that if they do not sleep, *El Coco* will come and get them. The rhyme originated in the 17th century has evolved over the years, but still retains its original meaning. Coconuts (Spanish: *coco*) received that name because their brownish hairy surface reminded Portuguese explorers of *coco*, a ghost with a pumpkin head. Latin America also has El Coco, although its folklore is usually quite different, commonly mixed with native beliefs, and, because of cultural contacts, sometimes more related to the boogeyman of the United States. However, the term *El Coco* is also used in Spanish-speaking Latin American countries, such as Bolivia, Colombia, Guatemala, Peru, Mexico, El Salvador, Honduras, the Dominican Republic, and Venezuela, although there it is more usually called *El Cuco*, as in Puerto Rico, Chile, Uruguay and Argentina. Among Mexican-Americans, *El Cucuy* is portrayed as an evil monster that hides under children's beds at night and kidnaps or eats the child that does not obey his/her parents or go to sleep when it is time to do so. However, the Spanish American bogeyman does not resemble the shapeless or hairy monster of Spain: social sciences professor Manuel Medrano says popular legend describes *El cucuy* as a small humanoid with glowing red eyes that hides in closets or under the bed. "Some lore has him as a kid who was the victim of violence... and now he's alive, but he's not," Medrano said, citing Xavier Garza's 2004 book *Creepy Creatures and other Cucuys*."[8]

In Brazilian folklore, a similar character called *Cuca* is depicted as a female humanoid alligator. There's a famous lullaby sung by most parents to their children that says that the *Cuca* will come and get them if they do not sleep, just as in Spain. The *Cuca* is also a character of Monteiro Lobato's *Sítio do Picapau Amarelo*, a series of short novels written for children which contain a large number of characters from Brazilian folklore.

Babau

In the countries of the eastern Mediterranean, children who misbehave are threatened with a creature known as "babau" (or "baubau", "baobao", "bavbav", or similar). In Italy and Romania, the Babau (in Romania, Bau-bau) is also called *l'uomo nero* (Romanian: *omul negru*) or "black man". In Italy, he is portrayed as a tall man wearing a heavy black coat, with a black hood or hat which hides his face. Sometimes, parents will knock loudly under the table, pretending that someone is knocking at the door, and say something like: "Here comes *l'uomo nero*! He must know that there's a child here who doesn't want to drink his soup!" *L'uomo nero* is not supposed to eat or harm children, just take them away to a mysterious and frightening place. A popular lullaby says that he would keep a child with him "for a whole year".[9] In Slovenia, the "Bavbav" is described as a formless spirit. In Greece and Cyprus, the equivalent of the Bogeyman is known as *Baboulas* (Greek: Μπαμπούλας). Typically, he is said to be hiding under the bed, although the details of his story is adapted by the parents in a variety of ways. In Egypt "al-Bu'bu'" (البعبع) is often depicted as a night creature dressed in black who haunts children that misbehave.

Butzemann

In Germanic countries, the bogeyman is called the *butzemann*, *busseman*, *buhman*, or *boeman*. In Germany, the bogeyman is known as the "Buhmann" or the *Butzemann*. The common German expression is "der schwarze Mann" ("the black man" in English), which refers to an inhuman creature

Hatred and confusion

Troy Williams

Donald Trump haters have gone to great lengths to enlighten the world about the flaws of America's new president and have also unwittingly exposed their hypocrisy.

Trump is a complicated man, and he won't be getting a nomination for sainthood anytime soon. He's arguably the most hated man in the world, but he's still our president.

Hate is one of the human's strongest emotions and differing opinions about Trump has America more divided than it has been in decades.

What's interesting is that many of those who hate him are not behaving any better themselves. The day after his inauguration hundreds of thousands of women marched in the anti-Trump demonstration in Washington D.C. They say he disrespects women. Based on what most of us have been exposed to about Trump, they probably have a legitimate point.

I know profanity and vulgarity have become more commonplace in our daily conversations, but when I heard women in anti-Trump speeches use that kind of language it made me wonder if they realized they were disrespecting themselves, too. Maybe I'm too old school, but I fail to see the need to use that kind of language to make a point.

The previous day during the inaugural ceremony there were daylong violent protests. In some areas near the ceremony, it was a full-scale riot, with some protesters smashing store windows, setting fires to trash cans, burning a limousine, and throwing bricks and concrete at the police. It was a dangerous day for the men and women in law enforcement.

And it didn't stop there. Some innocent civilians were assaulted because they came to the inauguration to support the president. For me, it was another one of those times when Democrats left me scratching my head. Where was the credible leadership? I kept waiting for someone to step up and denounce the violence, but DisruptJ20 participants, named after the date of the inauguration, was committed to shutting down peaceful celebrations and interfering with the rights of fellow citizens at all costs, even if it meant arrest.

I cannot imagine any reasonable person thinking this was OK, no matter what differences we have politically. All of this because the outcome of the election was not what some people expected or wanted. I understand President Trump not being their choice. What I don't understand is the over-the-top responses. In another instance, a senior woman on a flight from Baltimore to Seattle allegedly defecated a Trump fan seated next to her because. The Trump fan's crime was admitting that he "came to celebrate democracy." At President Trump's inauguration. When the woman understood his intent, she went on a vicious rant which led to her removal from the plane.

These trying times ought to cause all of us to examine ourselves. Scripture says, "Hypocrite! First take the log out of your eye, and then you will see clearly to take the speck out of your brother's eye."

Some of the activist politicians decided to boycott the inauguration. Most of the African American Democrats stayed home, primarily to show support for Hillary Clinton and many of their white colleagues attended. I was told by a Cumberland County Democratic Party insider that Hillary had to attend since she was a former first lady. And the strategy of blacks staying home and the whites going was to confuse the masses. Well, mission accomplished, because I was confused.

Was it a sensible move? Only time will tell. They didn't go and criticized anybody who wanted to go. Incredibly, it's reported that some entertainers were given death threats for choosing to perform. That's the backdrop to the media story about the attendance. There was a determined effort by Democrats to suppress the crowd, and the media is writing stories about how many people were there compared to President Obama's two inaugurations.

I understand President Trump not being their choice. What I don't understand is the over-the-top responses.

I received several messages on my Facebook page with a strategy to negatively affect the Nielsen rating of the event, as well. The scheme was to have all your television sets on all day on channels which would not broadcast the inauguration so as to suppress the ratings. Like President Bill Clinton said once, "It's the craziest thing I've ever seen," although he was referring to something else.

Some African Americans have become hypercritical of other blacks visiting and communicating with President Trump. Jim Brown, Steve Harvey and Martin Luther King III are three notable faces who have been subject to harsh criticism for just meeting with the man. Martin Luther King III met with Trump on the King national holiday, and some blacks were livid. A reasonable minded person might think that King, III, might be respected enough to represent what his father stood for and allowed to make an independent decision on visitation without checking in with the black leaders, but it's not so.

Maybe it's another scheme to confuse the masses.

Troy Williams is an independent management consultant. He is a WCLN Radio show co-host on Thursdays from 11 a.m. to noon. He can be reached at talktroywilliams@yahoo.com

Black American Leaders Since 1619

Map of Free and Slave States

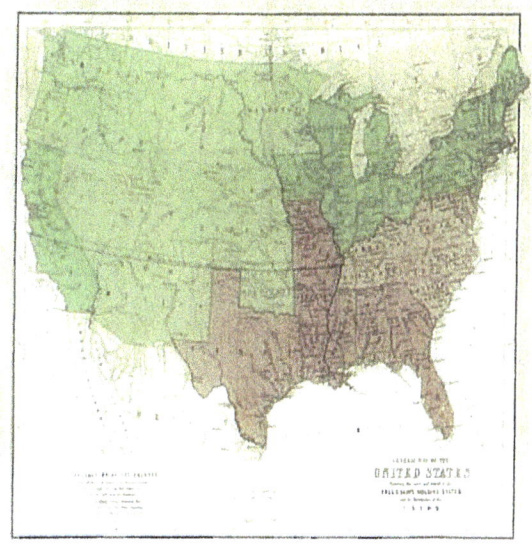

This is an original 1857 Map of the United States Showing the Free and Slave States. The Dark green states are the free states. The light green are the free "Territories", which were not yet states. The Red States were Slave Importing States, and the Pink States Were Slave States that Exported Slaves. Part of the dispute which helped trigger the Civil War was how to dispose of the territories — would they join the union as Slave or Free? The answer to this would tip the balance of power in the Congress, which is what made it such a difficult issue.

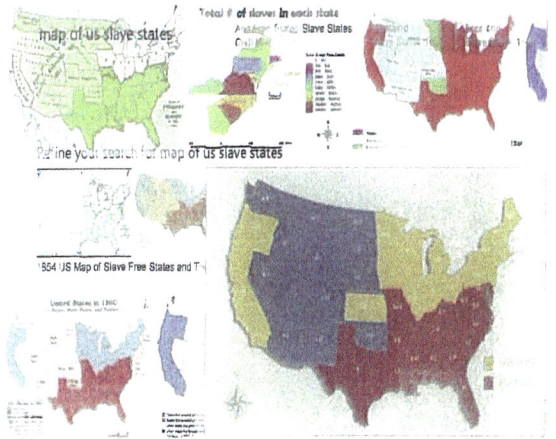

Africa During the Slave Trade

When the Portuguese began exploring the west coast of Africa, captain Dinis Dias came upon the Senegal River in 1444, the first great tropical river to be found by the Europeans, and by far the biggest that the Portuguese had encountered since leaving the Mediterranean. On the north bank of the river was the territory of the Azanaghi, a brown-skinned people, small and lean, of the Muslim faith. On the south bank the land was more fertile, covered with trees, and the people were black-skinned, tall and solidly built, belonging to the Wolof and Serer tribes. Farther south, Dias came upon a place, just north of Gorée island, where the coastline extended out far into the ocean. He named it Cabo Verde [2].

Africa consisted of a number of territories, many of them tribal regions. Each region had a form of government, religious beliefs, and traditions. Most had established some type of agriculture for food production. Occasionally, tribal wars would occur, and captives were taken as slaves. When the Europeans began trading for slaves, some of the tribes would war on other tribes or raid their villages with the objective of capturing slaves that could be bartered for European goods, including cloth, guns, gunpowder and horses.

Male Circumcision Ceremony, West Africa, 1728

Procession, including warriors with spears, musicians with drums, and houses in the background.

Muslim tribes in Northern and Western Africa performed circumcision for religious reasons. Elsewhere it was often considered a rite of passage into manhood. Circumcision ceremonies varied among the different tribes, but had much in common. A description of the Xhosa ceremony is given in

Mandingo Slave Traders and Coffle, Senegal, 1780's

Six African male slaves with two armed traders. The restraints consist of heavy pieces of wood, about 5 feet long, forked at one end. The fork fits around a slave's neck, and is secured with a large iron bolt that fits through holes drilled in the ends of the fork. Each slave carries on his shoulder the handle of the forked wood securing the slave behind him. The slaves are marched in single file in this fashion. Five or six armed traders could in this way transport as many as 50 slaves over great distances.

Gezo, King of Dahomey, 1849

King in regalia with one of his retainers holding umbrella.

In 1823 King Gezo liberated Dahomey from its subjection to the kingdom of Oyo, defeating them in battle. Today, Dahomey is known as Benin, where the largest ethnic group is the Fon tribe and closely related Adja and Ewe tribes. Oyo was located in what is now western Nigeria and its people belong to the Yoruba tribe.

In the 18th and 19th centuries, Dahomey was a major supplier of slaves to the Atlantic slave trade.

Yam Ceremony, Ashanti, 1817

Procession, King's retainers, and onlookers are shown at the annual yam ceremony, held just before the harvest. On the right, the King is seated under the state umbrella, with an elephant on top. The flags of Britain, Holland and Denmark are to the right and left of the throne.

Many tribes in West Africa have a yearly yam harvest festival. In the Igbo tradition (southeast Nigeria), newly harvested yams are offered to gods and dead ancestors before distributing them to villagers. This offering is made by the eldest male of the community or the king, who then eats the first yam of the harvest. The festival gives thanks to the spirits and gods who have helped achieve a plentiful harvest, important to the Igbo because yams represent life and survival. Yams from the previous year are disposed of to make room for the new crop.

nat turner's rebellion

Nat Turner

Nat Turner was an enslaved African American w[ho led a rebellion of]
slaves and free blacks in Southampton County, Virgi[nia in]
1831. The rebels went from plantat[ion] to [pl]antation [killing whites]
and guns, freeing othe[r] slaves along t[he way] and recr[uiting]
blacks who wanted to [join] their revol[t... ...]ng the rebelli[on]

Nat Turner

(1800–1831)

Nat Turner was the leader of a violent slave rebellion in Southampton County, Virginia, in 1831.

Synopsis

NAME
Nat Turner

BIRTH DATE
October 2, 1800

DEATH DATE
November 11, 1831

PLACE OF BIRTH
Southampton County, Virginia

PLACE OF DEATH
Jerusalem, Virginia

Nat Turner, born into slavery on October 2, 1800, on a Southampton County plantation, became a preacher who claimed he had been chosen by God to lead slaves from bondage. On August 21, 1831, he led a violent insurrection. He hid for six weeks but was eventually caught and later hanged. The incident ended the emancipation movement in that region and led to even harsher laws against slaves.

Early Life

Born on October 2, 1800, in Southampton County, Virginia, Nat Turner made history as the leader of one of the bloodiest slave revolts in America. He was born on the Virginia plantation of Benjamin Turner, who allowed him to be instructed in reading, writing, and religion. His mother was named Nancy, but nothing is known about his father.

As a small child, Turner was thought to have some special talent because he could describe things that happened before he was even born. Some even remarked that he "surely would be a prophet," according to his later confession. His mother and grandmother told Turner that he "was intended for some great purpose." Turner was deeply religious and spent much of his time reading the Bible, praying and fasting.

Nat Turner's slave rebellion

From Wikipedia, the free encyclopedia

Nat Turner's Rebellion (also known as the **Southampton Insurrection**) was a slave rebellion that took place in Southampton County, Virginia, during August 1831.[1] Led by Nat Turner, rebel slaves killed from 55 to 65 people, the highest number of fatalities caused by any slave uprising in the Southern United States. The rebellion was put down within a few days, but Turner survived in hiding for more than two months afterwards. The rebellion was effectively suppressed at Belmont Plantation on the morning of August 23, 1831.[2]

There was widespread fear in the aftermath of the rebellion, and white militias organized in retaliation against the slaves. The state executed 56 slaves accused of being part of the rebellion. In the frenzy, many non-participant slaves were punished. At least 100 African Americans, and possibly up to 200, were murdered by militias and mobs in the area. Across the South, state legislatures passed new laws prohibiting education of slaves and free black people,[3] restricting rights of assembly and other civil rights for free black people, and requiring white ministers to be present at all worship services.

Contents

- 1 Nat Turner's background
- 2 Rebellion
- 3 Retaliation
- 4 Aftermath
- 5 Legal response
- 6 See also
- 7 References
- 8 Sources
- 9 Further reading

Nat Turner's Slave Rebellion

1831 woodcut purporting to illustrate various stages of the rebellion.

Date	August 21–23, 1831
Location	Southampton County, Virginia
Result	Rebellion suppressed
	- Nat Turner tried, convicted, and hanged

Belligerents

Rebel slaves	United States
	- Local white militias

Commanders and leaders

Nat Turner

Casualties and losses

| 56 executed, 100–200 killed by militia and mobs | 55–65 killed |

North American slave revolts

Over the years, Turner worked on a number of different plantations. He ran away from Samuel Turner, his former owner's brother, in 1821. After thirty days hiding in the woods, Turner came back to Turner's plantation after he received what he believed to be a sign from God. After Samuel Turner's death, Nat Turner became the slave of Thomas Moore and then the property of his widow. When she married John Travis, Nat Turner went to work on Travis's lands.

Slave Rebellion Leader

Believing in signs and hearing divine voices, Turner had a vision in 1825 of a bloody conflict between black and white spirits. Three years later, he had what he believed to be another message from God. In his later confession, Turner explained "the Spirit instantly appeared to me and said the Serpent was loosened, and Christ had laid down the yoke he had borne for the sins of men, and that I should take it on and fight against the Serpent. " Turner would receive another sign to tell him when to fight, but this latest message meant "I should arise and prepare myself and slay my enemies with their own weapons."

Turner took a solar eclipse that occurred in February 1831 as a signal that the time to rise up had come. He recruited several other slaves to join him in his cause. On August 21, 1831, Turner and his supporters began their revolt against white slave owners with the killing the Travis family. Turner gathered more supporters—growing to a group of up to 40 or 50 slaves—as he and his men continued their violent spree through the county. They were able to secure arms and horses from those they killed. Most sources say that about 55 white men, women and children died during Turner's rebellion.

Initially Turner had planned to reach the county seat of Jerusalem and take over the armory there, but he and his men were foiled in this plan. They faced off against a group of armed white men at a plantation near Jerusalem, and the conflict soon dissolved into chaos. Turner himself fled into the woods.

Death and Legacy

While Turner hid away, white mobs took their revenge on the blacks of Southampton County. Estimates range from approximately 100 to 200 African Americans were slaughtered after the rebellion. Turner was eventually captured on October 30, 1831. He was represented by lawyer Thomas R. Gray, who wrote down Turner's confession. Turner pled not guilty during his trial, believing that his rebellion was the work of God. He was sentenced to death by hanging, and this sentence was carried out on November 11, 1831. Many of his co-conspirators met the same fate as Turner.

The incident put fear in the heart of southerners, ending the organized emancipation movement in that region. Southern states enacted even harsher laws against slaves instead. Turner's actions also added fuel to the abolitionist movement in the north. Noted abolitionist William Lloyd Garrison even published an editorial in his newspaper *The Liberator* in support of Turner to some degree.

Denmark Vesey

Civil Rights Activist (c. 1767–c. 1822)

Denmark Vesey was a freed slave who held meetings to organize what would have been the biggest slave revolt in U.S. history.

Synopsis

NAME
Denmark Vesey

OCCUPATION
Civil Rights Activist

BIRTH DATE
c. 1767

DEATH DATE
c. 1822

AKA
Telemaque

A slave, Denmark Vesey spent 20 years sailing with his master. In 1800 he purchased his freedom, took up carpentry and prospered at his trade. Although he would later deny it, he allegedly held meetings at his home to collect arms for an uprising he was planning for as many as 9,000 African Americans in South Carolina. The plan was betrayed by several fearful slaves and he and others were seized.

Profile

Insurrection leader. Probably born on St. Thomas, West Indies. The property of Captain Vesey, a Charleston, South Carolina, slave trader and planter, he spent 20 years sailing with his master. In 1800 he purchased his freedom (allegedly having won a lottery), took up carpentry in Charleston, and prospered at his trade.

By 1818 he was preaching to slaves at plantations throughout the region and, drawing on the Bible, he told them that, like the Israelites, they would gain their freedom. Although he would later deny it, he allegedly held meetings at his home to collect arms for an uprising he was planning for as many as 9000 African-Americans in South Carolina. The plan was betrayed by several fearful slaves and he and others were seized.

He defended himself ably at his trial, but was sentenced and hanged along with about 35 blacks; some 35 others were sold to West Indian plantation owners. It would have been the largest slave revolt in U.S. history, but its end result was the passing of even stricter laws against African-Americans.

Photographs of Slavery

Up | History of Slavery | Abraham Lincoln Entering Richmond Virginia | Slave Maps | Slave Ship | Slave Trader | Photographs of Slavery | African American Art | Uncle Tom's Cabin

Actual photographs of slaves and slave life are very rare. This makes sense . . . plantation owners and slave drivers certainly did not want to advertise and document their dark trade. After the slaves were freed, most were very poor and so did not have portraits made. We have done extensive research to find the few existing photos of slaves and ex-slaves. Below, for your consideration, we present these rare images of slaves and slave life. We are eager to expand this collection. If you are a descendent of a slave, and have images in a family album of someone who was a slave, we would be honored if you would share it with us, and the visitors to this site. Similarly, if you are the descendent of plantation or slave owners, we would be pleased if you would share your images.

Photographs of Slaves - Click on Image to be taken to a Larger Picture and Description

Old Slave in Overalls   Slave with his Dog   Slave on his Porch

Hands of a Slave   Slave Couple   Alabama Slave

Select source:

Ku Klux Klan

West's Encyclopedia of American Law
COPYRIGHT 2005 The Gale Group, Inc.

KU KLUX KLAN

Ku Klux Klan

Ku Klux Klan emblem

	In existence
1st Klan	1865–1870s
2nd Klan	1915–1944
3rd Klan	1946–present
	Members
1st Klan	Unknown
2nd Klan	3,000,000–6,000,000[1] (peaked in 1924–25)
3rd Klan	5,000–8,000[2]

The Ku Klux Klan (KKK) is a white supremacist organization that was founded in 1866. Throughout its notorious history, factions of the secret fraternal organization have used acts of terrorism—including murder, lynching, arson, rape, and bombing—to oppose the granting of civil rights to African Americans. Deriving its membership from native-born, white Protestant U.S. citizens, the KKK has also been anti-Semitic and anti-Catholic, and has opposed the immigration of all those it does not view as "racially pure."

Other names for the group have been White Brotherhood, Heroes of America, Constitutional Union Guards, and Invisible Empire.

Origins and Initial Growth

Ex-Confederate soldiers established the Ku Klux Klan in Pulaski, Tennessee, in 1866. They developed the first two words of the group's name from the Greek word *kuklos*, meaning "group or band," and took the third as a variant of the word *clan*. Starting as a largely recreational group, the Klan soon turned to intimidating newly freed African Americans. Riding at night, the Klan terrorized and sometimes murdered those it opposed. Members adopted a hooded white costume—a guise intended to represent the ghosts of the Confederate dead—to avoid identification and to frighten victims during nighttime raids.

The Klan fed off the post-Civil War resentments of white southerners—resentment that centered on the Reconstruction programs imposed on the South by a Republican Congress. Under Reconstruction, the North sought to restructure southern society on the basis of racial equality. Under this new regime, leading southern whites were disfranchised, while inexperienced African Americans, carpetbaggers (northerners who had migrated to the South following the war), and scalawags (southerners who cooperated with the North) occupied major political offices.

Shortly after the KKK's formation, Nathan Bedford Forrest, a former slave trader and Confederate general, assumed control of the organization and turned it into a militaristic, hierarchical entity. In 1868, Forrest formally disbanded the group after he became appalled by its growing violence. However, the KKK continued to grow, and its atrocities worsened. Drawing the core of its membership from ex-Confederate soldiers, the KKK may have numbered several hundred thousand at its height during Reconstruction.

In 1871, the federal government took a series of steps to counter the KKK and its violence. Congress organized a joint select committee made up of seven senators and 14 representatives to look into the Klan and its activities. It then passed the civil rights act of 1871, frequently referred to as the ku klux klan act, which made night-riding a crime and empowered the president to order the use of federal troops to put down conspirators by force. The law also provided criminal and civil penalties for people convicted of private conspiracies—such as those perpetrated by the KKK—intended to deny others their civil rights.

BLACK CODES

A body of laws, statutes, and rules enacted by southern states immediately after the Civil War to regain control over the freed slaves, maintain white supremacy, and ensure the continued supply of cheap labor.

The Union's victory over the South in the Civil War signaled the end for the institution of slavery in the United States. Ratified in 1865, the thirteenth amendment to the U.S. Constitution formalized this result in U.S. law, abolishing slavery throughout the country and every territory subject to its jurisdiction.

For the next several months, southern states sought a way to restore for the white majority what the Civil War and the Thirteenth Amendment had tried to deny them, supremacy, control, and economic power over the fate of African Americans. Under slavery, whites had disciplined the blacks largely outside the law, through extralegal whippings administered by slave owners and their overseers. After the slaves were emancipated, panicky whites feared that blacks would seek revenge against them for their harsh and inhumane treatment on the southern plantations. Former slave owners feared for themselves, their families, and their property.

BLACK CODES

BLACK CODES were the acts of legislation enacted in the Confederate states in 1865 and 1866 to limit the freedom of recently freed blacks. Some apply the term to Southern antebellum legislation that restricted the action and movements of slaves, although such laws are more frequently referred to as slave codes. Persons using the term "black codes" to include all such laws see the codes as originating in the seventeenth century, continuing until the Civil War, and being reenacted in slightly modified form immediately after the war.

The laws passed in 1865–1866 by the several states did extend some civil and legal rights to freed persons—permitting them to acquire and own property, marry, make contracts, sue and be sued, and testify in court cases involving persons of their own color. But the main purpose of the legislation was to stabilize the black workforce by compelling African Americans to work and by limiting their economic options. The codes typically had provisions for declaring blacks to be vagrants if they were un-employed and without permanent residence. As vagrants, they were subject to being arrested, fined, and bound out for a term of labor if unable to pay the fine. The codes also imposed penalties for refusing to complete a term of labor as well as for breaking an agreement to work when it was entered into voluntarily. Those who encouraged African Americans to refuse to abide by these restrictive laws were themselves subject to penalties. In like manner, black orphans could be apprenticed to work for a number of years. In many of these cases the whites to whom blacks were assigned turned out to be their former owners. The codes barred African Americans from testifying in court cases involving whites, often prohibited them from bearing firearms, and forbade intermarriage between the races. Of the states with the most restrictive legislation, Mississippi limited the types of property blacks could own, and South Carolina excluded blacks from certain businesses and from skilled trades.

While some white southerners thought that African-Americans were best controlled through vigilantism, Mississippi whites began passing laws to take away the former slaves' new found freedom. The first such law was enacted on November 22, 1865. It directed civil officers to hire orphaned African Americans and forbade the orphans to leave their place of employment for any reason. Orphans were typically compensated with a free place to live, free meals, and some type of nominal wage. Other white employers were prohibited from offering any enticement to blacks "employed" by someone else.

The Mississippi legislature next passed a vagrancy law, defining vagrants as workers who "neglected their calling or employment or misspent what they earned." Another Mississippi law required African Americans to carry with them written evidence of their present employment at all times, a practice that was hauntingly reminiscent of the old pass system under slavery. The final piece to the puzzle came when Mississippi established a system of special county courts to punish blacks charged with violating one of the new state employment laws. The law imposed draconian punishments, including "corporal chastisement" for blacks who refused to work or otherwise tried to frustrate the system. African Americans who committed real crimes, such as stealing, could be hung by their thumbs.

Widely considered to be the first set of *Black Codes* passed in the south after the Civil War, these Mississippi laws represented a concerted effort by white lawmakers to restore the master-slave relationship under a new name. Within a few months after Mississippi passed its first such law, Alabama, Georgia, Louisiana, Florida, Tennessee, Virginia, and North Carolina followed suit by enacting similar laws of their own.

Congress quickly responded to the Black Codes by passing the civil rights act of 1866, which made it illegal to discriminate against blacks by assigning them an inferior legal and economic status. Two years later the states ratified the fourteenth amendment, which guaranteed "equal protection of the laws" to the residents of every state.

But the southern states were not deterred. They soon passed a new set of laws that permitted local officials to informally discriminate against blacks, without specific statutory authority. The thrust-and-parry exchanges between Congress and the southern states continued throughout the period Reconstruction (1865-77) and through the first half of the twentieth century.

Jim Crow laws

From Wikipedia, the free encyclopedia

Jim Crow laws were state and local laws enforcing racial segregation in the Southern United States. Enacted after the Reconstruction period, these laws continued in force until 1965. They mandated *de jure* **racial segregation** in all public facilities in the states of the former Confederate States of America, starting in 1890 with a "separate but equal" status for African Americans. Facilities for African Americans were consistently inferior and underfunded compared to those available to European Americans; sometimes they did not exist at all. This body of law institutionalized a number of economic, educational, and social disadvantages. *De jure* segregation mainly applied to the Southern states, while Northern segregation was generally *de facto*—patterns of housing segregation enforced by private covenants, bank lending practices, and job discrimination, including discriminatory labor union practices.

Jim Crow laws—sometimes, as in Florida, part of state constitutions—mandated the segregation of public schools, public places, and public transportation, and the segregation of restrooms, restaurants, and drinking fountains for whites and blacks. The U.S. military was also segregated, as were federal workplaces, initiated in 1913 under President Woodrow Wilson. By requiring candidates to submit photos, his administration practiced racial discrimination in hiring.

Cover to an early edition of "Jump Jim Crow" sheet music (c. 1832)

These Jim Crow laws followed the 1800–1866 Black Codes, which had previously restricted the civil rights and civil liberties of African Americans. Segregation of public (state-sponsored) schools was declared unconstitutional by the Supreme Court of the United States in 1954 in *Brown v. Board of Education*, although in some cases it took years for this decision to be acted on. Generally, the remaining Jim Crow laws were overruled by the Civil Rights Act of 1964 and the Voting Rights Act of 1965, but years of action and court challenges were needed to unravel numerous means of institutional discrimination.

Etymology

The phrase "Jim Crow Law" can be found as early as 1892 in the title of a *New York Times* article about voting laws in the South.[1][2] The origin of the phrase "Jim Crow" has often been attributed to "Jump Jim Crow", a song-and-dance caricature of blacks performed by white actor Thomas D. Rice in blackface, which first surfaced in 1832 and was used to satirize Andrew Jackson's populist policies. As a result of Rice's fame, "Jim Crow" by 1838 had become a pejorative expression meaning "Negro". When southern legislatures passed laws of racial segregation which were directed against blacks at the end of the 19th century, these statutes became known as Jim Crow laws.[1]

Origins of Jim Crow laws

During the Reconstruction period of 1865–1877, federal laws provided civil rights protections in the U.S. South for freedmen, the African Americans who had formerly been slaves, and former free blacks. In the 1870s, Democrats gradually regained power in the Southern legislatures, having used insurgent paramilitary groups, such as the White League and the Red Shirts, to disrupt Republican organizing, run Republican officeholders out of town, and intimidate blacks to suppress their voting. Extensive voter fraud was also used. Gubernatorial elections were close and had been disputed in Louisiana for years, with increasing violence against blacks during campaigns from 1868 onward. In 1877, a national Democratic Party compromise to gain Southern support in the presidential election resulted in the government's withdrawing the last of the federal troops from the South. White Democrats had regained political power in every Southern state.[3] These Southern, white, Democratic Redeemer governments legislated Jim Crow laws officially segregating black people from the white population.

Freedmen voting in New Orleans, 1867

About.com   About Education   20th Century History   Civil Rights Around the World

Booker T. Washington
Black Educator and Founder of the Tuskegee Institute

Seated studio portrait of American educator, economist and industrialist Booker T. Washington (1856-1915), founder of the Tuskegee Institute in Alabama, early twentieth century. (Photo by Harris & Ewing/Interim Archives/Getty Images)

By Patricia Daniels, Contributing Writer

Who Was Booker T. Washington?

Booker T. Washington is best known as a prominent black educator and racial leader of the late 19th and early 20th centuries. He founded Tuskegee Institute in Alabama in 1881 and oversaw its growth into a well-respected black university.

Born into slavery, Washington rose to a position of power and influence among both blacks and whites. Although he earned the respect of many for his role in promoting education for blacks, Washington has also been criticized for being too accommodating to whites and too complacent on the issue of equal rights.

Dates: April 5, 1856[1] – November 14, 1915

Also Known As: Booker Taliaferro Washington; "The Great Accommodator"

Famous Quote: "No race can prosper till [sic] it learns that there is as much dignity in tilling a field as in writing a poem."

Early Childhood

Booker T. Washington was born in April 1856 on a small farm in Hale's Ford, Virginia. He was given the middle name "Taliaferro," but no last name.

His mother, Jane, was a slave and worked as the plantation cook. Based upon Booker's medium complexion and light gray eyes, historians have assumed that his father — whom he never knew — was a white man, possibly from a neighboring plantation. Booker had an older brother, John, also fathered by a white man.

Jane and her sons occupied a tiny one-room cabin with a dirt floor. Their dreary home lacked proper windows and had no beds for its occupants. Booker's family rarely had enough to eat and sometimes resorted to theft to supplement their meager provisions.

When Booker was about four years old, he was given small chores to do on the plantation. As he grew taller and stronger, his workload increased accordingly.

Around 1860, Jane married Washington Ferguson, a slave from a nearby plantation. Booker later took the first name of his stepfather as his own last name.

During the Civil War, the slaves on Booker's plantation, like many slaves in the South, continued to work for the owner even after the issuance of Lincoln's Emancipation Proclamation in 1863. By the end of the war, however, Booker T. Washington and his family were ready for a new opportunity.

In 1865, after the war ended, they moved to Malden, West Virginia, where Booker's stepfather had found a job as a salt packer for the local salt works.

Working in the Mines

Living conditions in their new home, located in a crowded and dirty neighborhood, were no better than those back at the plantation. Within days of their arrival, Booker and John were sent to work alongside their stepfather packing salt into barrels. Nine-year-old Booker despised the work, but found one benefit of the job: he learned to recognize his numbers by taking note of those written on the sides of the salt barrels.

Like many former slaves during the post-Civil War era, Booker longed to learn how to read and write. He was thrilled when his mother gave him a spelling book and soon taught himself the alphabet. When a black school opened in a nearby community, Booker begged to go, but his stepfather refused, insisting that the family needed the money he brought in from the salt packing. Booker eventually found a way to attend school at night.

When Booker was ten years old, his stepfather took him out of school and sent him to work in the nearby coal mines. Booker had been working there for nearly two years when an opportunity came along that would change his life for the better.

W. E. B. Du Bois

AMERICAN SOCIOLOGIST AND SOCIAL REFORMER

WRITTEN BY: Elliott Rudwick
LAST UPDATED: 12-17-2004 See Article History

Alternative Titles: William Edward Burghardt Du Bois, William Edward Burghardt DuBois

W. E. B. Du Bois, in full **William Edward Burghardt Du Bois** (born February 23, 1868, Great Barrington, Massachusetts, U.S.—died August 27, 1963, Accra, Ghana), American sociologist, the most important black protest leader in the United States during the first half of the 20th century. He shared in the creation of the National Association for the Advancement of Colored People (NAACP) in 1909 and edited *The Crisis*, its magazine, from 1910 to 1934. Late in life he became identified with communist causes.

W. E. B. Du Bois
AMERICAN SOCIOLOGIST AND SOCIAL REFORMER

ALSO KNOWN AS
William Edward Burghardt Du Bois
William Edward Burghardt DuBois

BORN
February 23, 1868
Great Barrington, Massachusetts

DIED
August 27, 1963
Accra, Ghana

W.E.B. Du Bois, 1918.
Courtesy of Atlanta University

W. E. B. Du Bois in 1918

Born	William Edward Burghardt Du Bois
February 23, 1868
Great Barrington, Massachusetts, United States
Died	August 27, 1963 (aged 95)
Accra, Ghana
Residence	Atlanta, Georgia
New York City, New York
Fields	Civil rights, sociology, history
Institutions	Atlanta University, NAACP
Alma mater	Fisk University
Harvard University
University of Berlin
Known for	*The Souls of Black Folk*
Black Reconstruction in America
The Crisis
Influences	Alexander Crummell
William James
Notable awards	Spingarn Medal (1920)
Lenin Peace Prize (1959)
Spouse	Nina Gomer Du Bois
Shirley Graham Du Bois
Signature	W.E.B.DuBois

Du Bois graduated from Fisk University, a black institution at Nashville, Tennessee, in 1888. He received a Ph.D. from Harvard University in 1895. His doctoral dissertation, *The Suppression of the African Slave-Trade to the United States of America, 1638-1870*, was published in 1896. Although Du Bois took an advanced degree in history, he was broadly trained in the social sciences; and, at a time when sociologists were theorizing about race relations, he was conducting empirical inquiries into the condition of blacks. For more than a decade he devoted himself to sociological investigations of blacks in America, producing 16 research monographs published between 1897 and 1914 at Atlanta (Georgia) University, where he was a professor, as well as *The Philadelphia Negro: A Social Study* (1899), the first case study of a black community in the United States.

W.E.B. Du Bois.
Library of Congress, Washington, D.C.

Although Du Bois had originally believed that social science could provide the knowledge to solve the race problem, he gradually came to the conclusion that in a climate of virulent racism, expressed in such evils as lynching, peonage, disfranchisement, Jim Crow segregation laws, and race riots, social change could be accomplished only through agitation and protest. In this view, he clashed with the most influential black leader of the period, Booker T. Washington, who, preaching a philosophy of accommodation, urged blacks to accept discrimination for the time being and elevate themselves through hard work and economic gain, thus winning the respect of the whites. In 1903, in his famous book *The Souls of Black Folk*, Du Bois charged that Washington's strategy, rather than freeing the black man from oppression, would serve only to perpetuate it. This attack crystallized the opposition to Booker T. Washington among many black intellectuals, polarizing the leaders of the black community into two wings—the "conservative" supporters of Washington and his radical critics.

MARCUS GARVEY

INTRODUCTION

Born in Jamaica, Marcus Garvey (1887-1940) became a leader in the black nationalist movement by applying the economic ideas of Pan-Africanists to the immense resources available in urban centers. After arriving in New York in 1916, he founded the Negro World newspaper, an international shipping company called Black Star Line and the Negro Factories Corporation. During the 1920s, his Universal Negro Improvement Association (UNIA) was the largest secular organization in African-American history. Indicted for mail fraud by the U.S. Justice Department in 1923, he spent two years in prison before being deported to Jamaica, and later died in London.

Garvey came to New York (/topics/us-states/new-york) in 1916 and concluded that the growing black communities in northern cities could provide the wealth and unity to end both imperialism in Africa and discrimination in the United States. He combined the economic nationalist ideas of Booker T. Washington (/topics/black-history/booker-t-washington) and Pan-Africanists with the political possibilities and urban style of men and women living outside of plantation and colonial societies.

Although local UNIA chapters provided many social and economic benefits for their members, Garvey's main efforts failed: the Black Star Line suspended operations in 1922 and the other enterprises fared no better. Garvey's ambition and determination to lead inevitably collided with associates and black leaders in other organizations. His verbal talent and flair for the dramatic attracted thousands, but his faltering projects only augmented ideological and personality conflicts. In the end, he could neither unite blacks nor accumulate enough power to significantly alter the societies the unia functioned in.

Finally, the Justice Department, animated by J. Edgar Hoover's Federal Bureau of Investigation and sensing his growing weakness, indicted Garvey for mail fraud. He was convicted in 1923, imprisoned in 1925, and deported to Jamaica in 1927. Unable to resurrect the unia, he moved to London, where he died in 1940.

Thurgood Marshall

From Wikipedia, the free encyclopedia

Thurgood Marshall (July 2, 1908 – January 24, 1993) was an Associate Justice of the Supreme Court of the United States, serving from October 1967 until October 1991. Marshall was the Court's 96th justice and its first African-American justice.

Before becoming a judge, Marshall was a lawyer who was best known for his high success rate in arguing before the Supreme Court and for the victory in *Brown v. Board of Education*, a decision that desegregated public schools. He served on the United States Court of Appeals for the Second Circuit after being appointed by President John F. Kennedy and then served as the Solicitor General after being appointed by President Lyndon Johnson in 1965. President Johnson nominated him to the United States Supreme Court in 1967.

Thurgood Marshall

Associate Justice of the Supreme Court of the United States

In office

October 2, 1967 – October 1, 1991[1]

Appointed by	Lyndon Johnson
Preceded by	Tom Clark
Succeeded by	Clarence Thomas

32nd Solicitor General of the United States

In office

August 23, 1965 – August 30, 1967

President	Lyndon Johnson
Preceded by	Archibald Cox
Succeeded by	Erwin Griswold

Judge of the United States Court of Appeals for the Second Circuit

In office

October 5, 1961 – August 23, 1965

Appointed by	John F. Kennedy
Preceded by	Seat established
Succeeded by	Wilfred Feinberg

Personal details

Born	July 2, 1908 Baltimore, Maryland, U.S.
Died	January 24, 1993 (aged 84) Bethesda, Maryland, U.S.

Contents

- 1 Early life
- 2 Law career
    - 2.1 Chief Counsel for the NAACP Legal Defense and Educational Fund
    - 2.2 Court of Appeals and Solicitor General
    - 2.3 U.S. Supreme Court
- 3 Death and legacy
- 4 Marriage and family
- 5 Thurgood Marshall Award
- 6 Timeline
- 7 Books authored
- 8 See also
- 9 Notes
- 10 Further reading
- 11 External links

Early life

Marshall was born in Baltimore, Maryland, on July 2, 1908. He was the great-grandson of a slave who was born in the modern-day Democratic Republic of the Congo;[2][3] his grandfather was also a slave.[4] His original name was Thoroughgood, but was eventually shortened to Thurgood in second grade because he disliked spelling it. His father, William Marshall, who was a railroad porter, and his mother Norma, a teacher, instilled in him an appreciation for the United States Constitution and the rule of law.[5]

Henry Highland Garnet School (P.S. 103), where Marshall attended elementary school

Marshall attended Frederick Douglass High School in Baltimore and was placed in the class with the best students. He graduated a year early in 1925 with a B-grade average, and placed in the top third of the class. Subsequently, he went to Lincoln University. It is commonly reported that he intended to study medicine and become a dentist.

Political party	Democratic
Spouse(s)	Buster Burey (1929–1955)
	Cecilia Suyat (1955–1993)
Children	Thurgood
	John
Alma mater	Lincoln University, Pennsylvania
	Howard University
Religion	Episcopalianism

But according to his application to Lincoln University,[6] Marshall stated that his goal was to become a lawyer. Among his classmates were poet Langston Hughes and musician Cab Calloway. Initially he did not take his studies seriously, and was suspended twice for hazing and pranks against fellow students.[7][8] He was not politically active at first, becoming a "star" of the debating team[8] and in his freshman year opposed the integration of African-American professors at the university.[7] Hughes later described him as "rough and ready, loud and wrong".[9] In his second year he got involved in a sit-in protest against segregation at a local movie theatre. In this same year, he was initiated as a member of the first black fraternity, Alpha Phi Alpha.[10] His marriage to Vivien Burey in September 1929 encouraged him to take his studies seriously, and he graduated from Lincoln with honors (*cum laude*) Bachelor of Arts in Humanities, with a major in American literature and philosophy.[8]

Marshall wanted to study in his hometown law school, the University of Maryland School of Law, but did not apply because of the school's segregation policy. Marshall instead attended Howard University School of Law, where he worked harder than he had at Lincoln and his views on discrimination were heavily influenced by the dean Charles Hamilton Houston.[8] In 1933, he graduated first in his class at Howard.[11]

Law career

After graduating from law school, Marshall started a private law practice in Baltimore. He began his 25-year affiliation with the National Association for the Advancement of Colored People (NAACP) in 1934 by representing the organization in the law school discrimination suit *Murray v. Pearson*. In 1936, Marshall became part of the national staff of the NAACP.[11]

In *Murray v. Pearson*, Marshall represented Donald Gaines Murray, a black Amherst College graduate with excellent credentials, who was denied admission to the University of Maryland Law School because of its segregation policy. Black students in Maryland wanting to study law had to attend segregated establishments, Morgan College, the Princess Anne Academy, or out-of-state black institutions. Using the strategy developed by Nathan Margold, Marshall argued that Maryland's segregation policy violated the "separate but equal" doctrine of *Plessy v. Ferguson* because the state did not provide a comparable educational opportunity at a state-run black institution.[12] The Maryland Court of Appeals ruled against the state of Maryland and its Attorney General, who represented the University of Maryland, stating, "Compliance with the Constitution cannot be deferred at the will of the state. Whatever system is adopted for legal education must furnish equality of treatment now."[13]

Thurgood Marshall in 1936 at the beginning of his career with the NAACP

54f. Martin Luther King Jr

Martin Luther King Jr.

King in 1964

1st President of the Southern Christian Leadership Conference

In office
Schools · Albany Movement · Birmingham campaign · Walk to Freedom · March on Washington for Jobs and Freedom · St. Augustine movement · Selma to Montgomery marches · Chicago Open Housing Movement · March Against Fear · Memphis sanitation strike · Poor People's Campaign

Death and memorial
Assassination · American federal holiday · National memorial

As the unquestioned leader of the peaceful Civil Rights Movement in the 1960s, **DR. MARTIN LUTHER KING JR.** was at the same time one of the most beloved and one of the most hated men of his time. From his involvement in the Montgomery bus boycott in 1955 until his untimely death in 1968, King's message of change through peaceful means added to the movement's numbers and gave it its moral strength. The legacy of Martin Luther King Jr. is embodied in these two simple words: equality and nonviolence.

King was raised in an activist family. His father was deeply influenced by **MARCUS GARVEY'S BACK TO AFRICA MOVEMENT** in the 1920s. His mother was the daughter of one of Atlanta's most influential African American ministers. As a student, King excelled. He easily moved through grade levels and entered Morehouse College, his father's alma mater, at the age of fifteen. Next, he attended Crozer Theological Seminary, where he received a Bachelor of Divinity degree. While he was pursuing his doctorate at Boston University, he met and married **CORETTA SCOTT**. After receiving his Ph.D. in 1955, King accepted an appointment to the Dexter Street Baptist Church in Montgomery, Alabama.

The high school that King attended was named after African-American educator Booker T. Washington.

After his organization of the bus boycott, King formed the Southern Christian Leadership Conference, which dedicated itself to the advancement of rights for African Americans. In April 1963, King

Birmingham, Alabama, police commissioner Bull Connor ordered that fire hoses and dogs be used to subdue protesters. The violence that ensued was broadcast across the nation galvanized the Civil Rights Movement.

organized a protest in Birmingham, Alabama, a city King called "the most thoroughly segregated city in the United States." Since the end of World War II, there had been 60 unsolved bombings of African American churches and homes.

Boycotts, sit-ins and marches were conducted. When Bull Connor, head of the Birmingham police department, used fire hoses and dogs on the demonstrators, millions saw the images on television. King was arrested. But support came from around the nation and the world for King and his family. Later in 1963, he delivered his famous "I Have a Dream" speech to thousands in Washington, D.C.

After the passage of the Civil Rights Act of 1964, King turned his efforts to registering African American voters in the South. In 1965, he led a march in Selma, Alabama, to increase the percentage of African American voters in Alabama. Again, King was arrested. Again, the marchers faced attacks by the police. Tear gas, cattle prods, and billy clubs fell on the peaceful demonstrators. Public opinion weighed predominantly on the side of King and the protesters. Finally, President Johnson ordered the National Guard to protect the demonstrators from attack, and King was able to complete the long march from Selma to the state capital of Montgomery. The action in Selma led to the passage of the Voting Rights Act of 1965.

In March 1965, Dr. King led protestors on a 50-mile, voting-rights march from Selma to Montgomery, Alabama. It took three attempts for the protestors to complete the march, battling tear gas, cattle prods, and police batons, but the national attention drawn by their efforts ultimately led to the Voting Rights Act of 1965.

Early in the morning of April 4, 1968, King was shot by **JAMES EARL RAY**. Spontaneous violence spread through urban areas as mourners unleashed their rage at the loss of their leader. Rioting burst forth in many American cities.

Malcolm X

From Wikipedia, the free encyclopedia

Malcolm X (/ˈmælkəm ˈɛks/; May 19, 1925 – February 21, 1965), born **Malcolm Little** and later also known as **el-Hajj Malik el-Shabazz**[A] (Arabic: الحاج مالك الشباز), was an African-American Muslim minister and human rights activist. To his admirers he was a courageous advocate for the rights of blacks, a man who indicted white America in the harshest terms for its crimes against black Americans; detractors accused him of preaching racism and violence. He has been called one of the greatest and most influential African Americans in history.

Malcolm X was effectively orphaned early in life. His father was killed when he was six and his mother was placed in a mental hospital when he was thirteen, after which he lived in a series of foster homes. In 1946, at age 20, he went to prison for larceny and breaking and entering. While in prison, Malcolm X became a member of the Nation of Islam, and after his parole in 1952, quickly rose to become one of the organization's most influential leaders. He served as the public face of the controversial group for a dozen years. In his autobiography, Malcolm X wrote proudly of some of the social achievements the Nation made while he was a member, particularly its free drug rehabilitation program. The Nation promoted black supremacy, advocated the separation of black and white Americans, and rejected the civil rights movement for its emphasis on integration.

By March 1964, Malcolm X had grown disillusioned with the Nation of Islam and its leader Elijah Muhammad. Expressing many regrets about his time with them, which he had come to regard as largely wasted, he embraced Sunni Islam. After a period of travel in Africa and the Middle East, which included completing the Hajj, he repudiated the Nation of Islam, disavowed racism and founded Muslim Mosque, Inc. and the Organization of Afro-American Unity. He continued to emphasize Pan-Africanism, black self-determination, and black self-defense. In February 1965, he was assassinated by three members of the Nation of Islam.

Malcolm X

Malcolm X in March 1964

Born	Malcolm Little May 19, 1925 Omaha, Nebraska
Died	February 21, 1965 (aged 39) Manhattan, New York
Cause of death	Assassination (multiple gunshots)
Resting place	Ferncliff Cemetery
Other names	el-Hajj Malik el-Shabazz (الحاج مالك الشباز)
Occupation	Minister, activist
Organization	Nation of Islam, Muslim Mosque, Inc., Organization of Afro-American Unity
Movement	Black nationalism, Pan-Africanism
Spouse(s)	Betty Shabazz (m. 1958–65)

Early years

Malcolm Little was born May 19, 1925, in Omaha, Nebraska, the fourth of seven children of Grenada-born Louise Helen Little (née Norton) and Georgia-born Earl Little.[1] Earl was an outspoken Baptist lay speaker, and he and Louise were admirers of Pan-African activist Marcus Garvey. Earl was local leader of the Universal Negro Improvement Association (UNIA) and Louise served as secretary and "branch reporter", sending news of local UNIA activities to *Negro World*; they inculcated self-reliance and black pride in their children.[2][3][4] Malcolm X later said that white violence killed three of his father's brothers.[5]

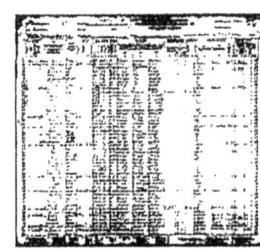

1930 United States Census return listing the Little family (lines 59ff.)

Because of Ku Klux Klan threats—Earl's UNIA activities were "spreading trouble"[6]—the family relocated in 1926 to Milwaukee, Wisconsin, and shortly thereafter to Lansing, Michigan.[7] There the family was frequently harassed by the Black Legion, a white racist group. When the family home burned in 1929, Earl accused the Black Legion.[8]

When Little was six, his father died in what was officially ruled a streetcar accident, though his mother Louise believed Earl had been murdered by the Black Legion. Rumors that white racists were responsible for his father's death were widely circulated, and were very disturbing to Malcolm X as a child. As an adult, he expressed conflicting beliefs on the question.[9] After a dispute with creditors, Louise received a life insurance benefit (nominally $1,000—about $16,000 in 2016 dollars[B]) in payments of $18 per month;[10] the issuer of another, larger policy refused to pay, claiming her husband Earl had committed suicide.[11] To make ends meet Louise rented out part of her garden, and her sons hunted game.[12]

In 1937 a man Louise had been dating—marriage had seemed a possibility—vanished from her life when she became pregnant with his child.[13] In late 1938 she had a nervous breakdown and was committed to Kalamazoo State Hospital. The children were separated and sent to foster homes. Malcolm and his siblings secured her release 24 years later.[14][15]

Freedom [1] in World History

Study of these earliest known civilizations:

- Sumerian - 3200-2360 B.C.
- Egyptian - 2850-715 B.C.
- Minoan - 2600-1400 B.C.
- Mesopotamian - 2500-1700 B.C.
- Indus - 2500 - 1800 B.C.
- Shang - 1525 - 1028 B.C

reveals that freedom was generally limited to those people at the top of the social pyramid:
- People with money enough to buy or control others
- Priests or political-economic rulers, with knowledge of how to manipulate others

> As humans abandoned the life of wandering, tribal hunters and learned to till the soil, they needed to predict the seasons. Special knowledge was required in order to know when to plant, when to expect floods in fertile valleys, when to expect rainy seasons, and when to reap the crops. Humans had not yet invented the calendar. The first humans who discovered the regularities of sun, moon, and stars that presage the seasons possessed powerful knowledge. Many of these humans used their knowledge to manipulate and control their credulous fellow humans. For example, knowing from astronomical observations when the rainy season would occur and begin the floods, they

pretended that they could control the gods and bring down the rains.

The early occult astronomical priesthoods, such as the designers of Stonehenge, convinced their subjects that they alone had contact with the gods. Thus only they could assure the return of the life-giving rains and bountiful harvests. Since they knew when solar and lunar eclipses would occur, they pretended that they actually *caused* such wonders by controlling the gods. When predictions (called priestly magic) sometimes went awry, the priests claimed that these resulted from the people's sins. The priests demanded that the people worship them or their gods and give them of their substance, including their most beautiful daughters.

As various trades developed, their practices and knowledge were kept secret. Mathematics, for example, became an arcane science, known only to a few. The knowledge of how to construct buildings - masonry and carpentry - became secrets arts and later played a part in concealed rituals in secret societies such as Masonry. A person would gain power through military skill or special knowledge, and assume the role of ruler. In many instances, this person would make their subjects believe that the gods had decreed their rule.

In the era of these ancient 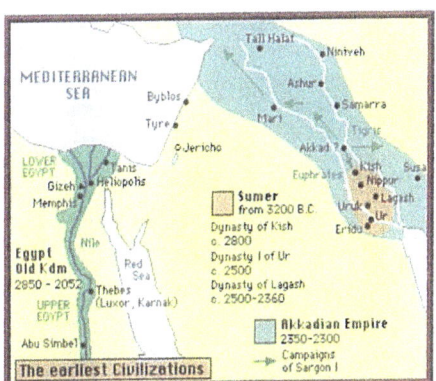 civilizations, freedom for the common person fluctuated, depending on the will of the specific ruler or ruling dynasty in power. The division of humans into classes, slavery, and the "divine right of rulers" were unquestioned cultural presuppositions. At times, an enlightened ruler might establish rule by law, protection of the weak, and general economic prosperity for all classes. But most of world history involves ego-maniacal, power-mad rulers enslaving the common people and waging protracted war against all other rulers.

 During the latter history of the Egyptian culture the Theban god, Amun, and the ancient Egyptian dynastic divinity, Re, were merged, resulting in changes in religious and social beliefs and practices. The exclusive

 royal privilege of immortality vanished; every Egyptian was assured of his own personal survival after death. For a brief period, common Egyptian people enjoyed the freedom of owning their own parcel of land and following the trade of their choice. Trade secrets were no longer kept.

The Babylonian ruler Hammurabi (1711-1669 B.C.) established a Code by which his kingdom was ruled, assured justice for the weak, and brought economic prosperity to his people. The stele to the left shows the god of justice, Shamash, dictating his laws to Hammurabi.

The Israelite people established a nation-state ruled at various times by kings, priests, and judges. They established their own legal code based on religious dogmas and, in part, the Code of Hammurabi.

The ruling powers tended to adopt one or a combination of these:

- Plutocracy - rule through wealth
- Militarism - rule through military power
- Sacerdotalism - rule through religious dogma and practice
- Oligarchy - rule through a small cabal

In general, the common people enjoyed little if any freedom, serving at the behest of their rulers. The rulers kept their subjects under control through conditioning them with religions which sanctioned the ruler's power. Common people were forced to work at mind- and body-destroying jobs which gave them no time or energy for reflective thought or unified reform activities.

---

[1] Freedom
Herbert J. Muller's definition of freedom is one of the most comprehensive: (1964). *Freedom in the Western World: From the Dark Ages to the Rise of Democracy*

> "I am adhering to the broad but relatively neutral definition of freedom as 'the condition of being able to choose and carry out purposes.' This includes the most common meaning of the absence of external constraints, or freedom from coercion; the idea of actual ability with available means, or effective freedom to do what one wishes; and the assumption of a power of deliberate choice between known alternatives, involving freedom of mind and spirit, which is hardest to specify but still distinguishes human freedom from the ability of other animals to carry out their instinctive purposes. In the words of Christian Bay, 'A person is free to the extent that he has the capacity, the opportunity, and the incentive to give expression to what is in him and to develop his potentialities.'

U.S. Freedoms

Declaration of Independence

We hold these Truths to be self-evident, that all Men are created equal, that they are endowed, by their Creator, with certain unalienable Rights, that among these are Life, Liberty, and the Pursuit of Happiness.

That to secure these Rights, Governments are instituted among Men, deriving their just Powers from the Consent of the Governed, that whenever any Form of Government becomes destructive of these Ends, it is the Right of the People to alter or abolish it, and to institute new Government, laying its Foundation on such Principles, and organizing its Powers in such Form, as to them shall seem most likely to effect their Safety and Happiness.

- Drafted on June 11, 1776
- Ratified on July 4, 1776
- Signed on August 2, 1776

U.S. Constitution

We the People of the United States, in Order to form a more perfect Union, establish Justice, insure domestic Tranquility, provide for the common defence, promote the general Welfare, and secure the Blessings of Liberty to ourselves and our Posterity, do ordain and establish this Constitution for the United States of America.

Consists of seven articles
1. Legislative power
2. Executive power
3. Judicial power
4. States' powers and limits
5. Process of amendment
6. Federal power
7. Ratification

- Completed on September 17, 1787
- Took effect on March 4, 1789

Bill of Rights

Consists of ten amendments

1. Freedom of speech, press, religion, peaceable assembly, and to petition the government
2. Right to keep and bear arms
3. Protection from quartering of troops
4. Protection from unreasonable search and seizure
5. Due process, double jeopardy, self-incrimination, private property
6. Trial by jury and other rights of the accused.
7. Civil trial by jury
8. Prohibition of excessive bail, as well as cruel or

US Supreme Court, Recent decisions

» LIGHTFOOT CRYSTAL M., ET AL. v. CENDANT MORTGAGE CORP., ET AL. Decided 01/18/2017
» WHITE v. PAULY. Decided 01/09/2017

Deeplinks

» A School Librarian Caught In The Middle of Student Privacy Extremes
» YODA, the Bill That Would Let You Own (and Sell) Your Devices, Is Re-Introduced in Congress
» The Fight Over Email Privacy Moves to the Senate
» It's the End of the Copyright Alert System (As We Know It)
» Documents About Financial Censorship Under Operation Choke Point Show Concern from Congress, Provide Few Answers
» EFF to Supreme Court: Patent Holders

unusual punishment
9. Protection of rights not specifically enumerated in the Bill of Rights
10. Powers of states and people

- Took effect on December 15, 1791

Explore your freedoms
» National Archives - Charters of Freedom
» Library of Congress - THOMAS
» U.S. Constitution with Annotations

Organizations
» ALA - Office for Intellectual Freedom
» American Civil Liberties Union
» Electronic Frontier Foundation
» Electronic Privacy Information Center
» National Coalition Against Censorship
» Center for Democracy & Technology
» First Amendment Center
» Bill of Rights Defense Committee

The Courts
» Supreme Court of the United States
» FindLaw - Supreme Court Center
» OYEZ - U.S. Supreme Court Multimedia
» Duke Law - Supreme Court Online
» Cornell Law - Supreme Court Collection
» U.S. Courts - The Federal Judiciary

Legal Research
» FindLaw
» LexisNexis
» Westlaw
» First Amendment Library

American Civil Liberties Union
» Social Networking Powerhouse Facebook Steps Forward to Bar Discriminatory Advertising on Its Site
» ACLU and Other Groups Ask for Emergency Hearing on the Muslim Ban from International Human Rights Body
» This Supreme Court Case Could Affect Trans Lives for Generations
» New Documents Show This TSA Program Blamed for Profiling Is Unscientific and Unreliable — But Still It Continues
» Donald Trump's Pick for the EPA Is Stonewalling on Releasing Records Linking Him to the Fossil Fuel Industry, So We're Suing for His Compliance
» ACLU Announces Expansion Plan to Fight Trump Policies
» Flying Home From Abroad, a Border Agent Stopped and Questioned Me ...

Shouldn't Be Allowed to Cherry Pick the Courts
» Violating Terms of Use Isn't a Crime, EFF Tells Court—Again

Slashdot: Your Rights Online
» Police Arrest Five Men For Selling Kodi Boxes 'Fully Loaded' With Illegal Streaming Apps
» Intel To Invest $7 Billion In Factory In Arizona, Employ 3,000 People
» Why Has Cameroon Blocked the Internet?
» Microsoft Now Offers Patent Troll Defense For Azure Customers
» US Visitors May Have to Hand Over Social Media Passwords: DHS
» NYC Fines Airbnb Hosts For 'Illegal' Home Rentals
» There Are Now Twice As Many Solar Jobs As Coal Jobs In the US

What Does "Freedom" Mean?

Richard Salbato - May 4, 1009

My latest Newsletter, "Dignity & St. Joseph, the Worker" prompted such a large response (100% good) that I have decided to expand on the theme of dignity. As expressed in the last article we are born with dignity and we or others can do nothing to add to our dignity as humans, but can only take away that dignity by failing to live up to it.

The two major reasons for this dignity are that fact that we have free will and can never die. These are the two reasons we are made in the image and likeness of God. We will expand now on the meaning of free-will. Free-will means that we have the freedom to choose good and evil, truth and falsehood, love and hate, and/or peace and war.

All this implies that we have the freedom to choose, and so, freedom is the subject here. We know from the above that God gave us freedom, but what does this word mean? How do we protect our freedom? How do we use it for our selves and the common good? Should we give up some freedom for the better good of all?

The enemy of freedom is **force, coercion and/or psychological aggression**. These enemies of freedom are not the same as the consequences of using freedom badly. God does not force us to do anything, but He does have consequences for choosing evil over good. Consequences are always there when we choose the good or the evil. These consequences are even there if we lived alone in a cave all the days of our life. Nevertheless, we still are not forced to do this or that.

When we are forced to do anything, we have lost our freedom. Totalitarian governments take all freedoms from all the people except themselves. Anarchy gives individuals total freedom, but does not protect the weak from the strong. Democracies give freedom to the majority, but not the minority. Pure Capitalism gives freedom to the rich but not to the poor. More on this later!

False Freedom

There is no limit to the sophisms by which the attractions of the word 'freedom' can be used to support measures which destroy individual freedom, no end to the tricks by which people can be exhorted in the name of freedom to give up their freedom.

Liberal do-gooders have tried to expand the meaning of "Freedom" to include freedom from poverty, starvation, treatable disease, and even from making the wrong choices. "Liberty" and "freedom" have probably been the most abused words in recent history.

This false idea of freedom takes away the freedom to fail and suffer the consequences of failure. This false idea of freedom takes away freedom. In order to reward failure, government has to take from the successful and give to those who failed, and do so without their permission. In other words, forced charity, and force is not freedom.

What right does a man have to free medical care, who spends 20% of his income on beer but nothing on health care insurance. You could solve the uninsured just by making insurance mandatory, just like driver's insurance. It would cost the tax-payers nothing.

The unforeseen consequence of this false idea of freedom is what breeds and rewards failure and failure fails. Even governments fail and many have. I would not be against this government failing, because people would wake up and build a better nation. **(Note One)**

Government's First Job

The first job of a good government is to protect freedom and in order to do this it must be the regulator of equal fairness and justice – fairness and justice for all. All authority, in Churches, Governments, or Family must be **protectors of the rule of law** just like sports games.

Imagine a basket ball game without rules, and referees to enforce these rules. In order to give equal opportunity for two teams to win or loose a game, we first must have equal rules and someone to enforce these rules. It takes very little money to pass rules of fairness and enforce them.

When the rules of fairness in sports are found to be unequal, new laws are passed to equalize the game. The same was true in America's government in the past, when it found that Colored People were not being treated equal we went to war. When it found that rich people were monopolizing a section of the economy and eliminating the fairness of competition, it outlawed unfair monopolies and even broke up large companies.

It was always interesting to me that the richest people in America are Democrats, whereas the rich (but not very rich people) are Republicans. The reason for this is the very, very rich get unfair advantages that make them filthy rich. It is like a referee that calls a game hard on one side but easy on the other. This is why the IRS code is 10,000 pages long, so that the filthy rich have an advantage over the smaller businesses.

When the government gives billions of dollars to failed banks, they create an unfair advantage to the big banks over the smaller banks. When it is not fair, it is not freedom. Allowing them to be so big in the first place was not in the interests of fairness and justice, therefore it is not true freedom.

It was this government's unfair refereeing that caused all the recessions and depressions of this country. This recession was because the governments gave big banks and FM and FM unfair advantages over the free market, which created the bubble. Now to correct the government's own mistake, they want to take 30% more of our freedom to bail them out.

The next bailout will be **Cap and Trade**. Spain has had Cap and Trade for 10 years and the green jobs have cost them $500,000 per job and ended with a net loss of jobs so that for every green job there were 3 jobs lost. Now they have unemployment of 17.5%.

Pure Capitalism does not work

If pure capitalism were allowed like many want (Libertarians), it would be like a basketball game with no rules and no referees. Capitalism, with rules and regulations to make competition equal and fair is the greatest system in the world. Without the rule of law and regulations for justice and equality, it becomes no better than Socialism. Every social system that works depends on justice and fairness.

We still today do not have a proper Capitalism with fairness in America, because we do not have equal fairness in the unions, especially in the Government unions. The founder of unions in America was against monopolies, and he knew that unions could also become monopolies, and so he advised that unions should never become larger than the companies they were in or the town. Today we have unions that cover hundreds of businesses but they have no competition because they have pushed out everyone else and the government did nothing. The teacher's union should not be larger than the city it is in but it covers the entire USA.

The fundamental danger to political or financial freedom is the concentration of power. The existence of a large measure of power in the hands of a relatively few individuals (government, business or unions) enables them to use it to coerce their fellow men.

Preservation of freedom requires either the elimination of power where that is possible or its dispersal where it cannot be eliminated.

Freedom in our daily life

As said above, God does not take away our free-will - our freedom to choose right and wrong. But He informs us of the consequences of these choices. In the same way we should kindly inform our children or friends of the consequences of our freedom to choose, but we should never force them to the point they have no freedom. "You do not like the rules; you have the freedom to leave. – You do not want to study; you have the freedom to fail. – You do not want to work; you have the freedom to be poor. – I am not going to reward you for choosing poorly."

www.ingramcontent.com/pod-product-compliance
Lightning Source LLC
Chambersburg PA
CBHW061358010526
44107CB00012B/974